Welcome to the Journey!

Oh, the depth of the riches both of the wisdom

and knowledge of God! How unsearchable are

His judgments and unfathomable His ways!

For who has known the mind of the Lord,

or who became His counselor?" ...For from

Him and through Him and to Him are

all things to Him be the glory forever. Amen.

— ROMANS 11:33-34, 36

WALK
THRU THE
BIBLE

GOD: AS HE LONGS FOR YOU TO SEE HIM JOURNAL

Produced with the assistance of Nightglass Media Group, Brian Goins & Dona Cohan Designs. Walk Thru the Bible project staff includes: Aisha Arbuckle, Dave Ball, Bethany Graham, Rebecca Gregory, Bradley Tomlinson, and Hayley Walthall.

GOD

AS HE LONGS FOR YOU TO SEE HIM

"Our aim in studying the Godhead must be to know God Himself better. Our concern must be to enlarge our acquaintance, not simply with the doctrine of God's attributes, but with the living God whose attributes they are."

— J. I. Packer

"I know nothing which can so comfort the soul; so calm the swelling billows of sorrow and grief; so speak peace to the winds of trial, as a devout musing upon the subject of the Godhead."

— C. S. Lewis

 **VIDEO NOTES**

How this study works

During the week:
~ Read or listen to the chapter assigned for that week
~ Complete the corresponding journal questions and/or activities

During the group time:
~ Watch the video
~ Be ready to discuss

Small Group Questions

1. When you think of God's existence, how do you perceive the culture is thinking about Him? What do you think other people are thinking about when they ponder God?

2. If you were forced to describe God with one word, what word would you use and why?

3. Share with the group one thing you are hoping to get out of this study.

 From Head to Heart

Think of someone in your circle (maybe at the office, in the neighborhood, or at your school) and let them know you are studying the existence of God. With no pressure, ask them the first two questions above. Report the responses to the group. You may find the answers surprising.

1. Confidentiality – *What is said in the group stays in the group. Let's assure each other that everyone is safe to share.*

2. No pressure – *Everyone has the option to pass. In fact it's best not to go in a circle every time to answer questions. Share "popcorn style." Allow people to speak as they are led.*

3. Care for one another – *This is not a teaching session as much as it is an opportunity to love and care for others. Pray for each other during the week. Find ways to check in on people in your group.*

GOD

AS HE LONGS FOR
YOU TO SEE HIM

God: As He Longs for You to See Him

I

WEEK ONE

Seeing God with 20/20 Vision

Grandfather in a rocking chair.

Cosmic cop.

Blind watchmaker.

What's your picture of God? Does He smile down at us with a wink and a nod? Does He wait to pounce when we break his laws? Did He wind up the universe and move on to the next galaxy? Even if it's an empty frame, we all have our own portrait of this entity known more commonly as God.

A. W. Tozer, an American pastor and writer during the 20th century, wrote, "What comes into our minds when we think about God is the most important thing about us." How we see God will determine in large part how we view ourselves. Are we loved? Are we under scrutiny? Does anyone really care?

There are two crucial questions we must answer: what is our perception of God and is it right? Like viewing God through distorted lenses, many of us make three common mistakes when we imagine what God looks like:

- ⁓ We tend to assume that God is just like us.
- ⁓ We tend to reduce Him to measurable and controllable terms.
- ⁓ We tend to overlook the obvious and significant ways that He has revealed Himself to us.

Nothing in all your life will impact your relationship with God, your relationship with people, your self-view, your decisions, and your purpose like the way you think of God. This week we start with a profound truth: He wants you to see Him clearly.

Day 1 ~

Read chapters 1-2 in *God: As He Longs for You to See Him*. What have been some of your misperceptions of God? How has that affected the way you live?

> *"What you think about God shapes your whole relationship with Him. In addition, what you believe God thinks about you determines how close you will grow toward Him."*
>
> — Chip

_____

_____

_____

_____

_____

_____

_____

_____

_____

_____

_____

_____

_____

_____

_____

_____

_____

_____

_____

_____

_____

_____

_____

_____

Day 2 ~

What do you think God thinks about you? How do these perceptions affect your relationship with Him?

But whatever things were gain to me, those things I have counted as loss for the sake of Christ. More than that, I count all things to be loss in view of the surpassing value of knowing Christ Jesus my Lord, for whom I have suffered the loss of all things, and count them but rubbish so that I may gain Christ, and may be found in Him, not having a righteousness of my own derived from the law, but that which is through faith in Christ, the righteousness which comes from God on the basis of faith, that I may know Him and the power of His resurrection and the fellowship of His sufferings, being conformed to His death ...

— Philippians 3: 7-10

Day 3 ~

RENEW YOUR MIND

Our vision of who God is can be improved by a clear picture from His Word. Take a moment today to memorize and meditate on this verse:

> The Lord your God is in your midst,
> a victorious warrior
>   He will exult over you with joy,
>   He will be quiet in His love,
>   He will rejoice over you with shouts of joy.
>
> — Zephaniah 3:17

"As much as it is humanly possible, we must get an accurate, clear picture of who the Creator of the universe is and exactly what He is like...And here's the motivation: until you know God as He is, you'll never become all that He's created you to be."

— Chip

Day 4 ~

Read chapter 3 in *God: As He Longs for You to See Him*. Did you take a moment to stop for a few minutes and think about who God is and what He is like? Reflect on the character of God and your desire to know Him. Give your heart, soul, and mind an opportunity to consider who made you, who loves you, and who longs to be seen clearly by you. At the end, spend a few minutes in prayer with Him. Ask Him to reveal Himself to you.

"We tend by a secret law of the soul to move toward our mental image of God."

— A. W. Tozer

Day 5 ~

God has revealed Himself in many different ways throughout Scripture. Look at each one of the verses below and describe how God specifically manifested Himself to us.

Psalm 19

_____

_____

_____

John 1:1-4; 14

_____

_____

_____

John 1:17-18; Hebrews 1:3

_____

_____

_____

Read chapter 1
in A. W. Tozer's _Knowledge of the Holy._

Tools for
Life Change:

There are two books we recommend that will give additional insight as you continue your journey on the attributes of God. Please consider adding, A. W. Tozer's **Knowledge of the Holy** _and J. I. Packer's_ **Knowing God** _to your library._

Is Your God too Small?

Where were you when I laid the foundation of the earth?
Tell Me, if you have understanding...   — Job 38:4

"How may we form a right idea of God's greatness? First *is to remove from our thoughts of God limits that would make Him small.* The second *is to compare Him with powers and forces which we regard as great.*"

— J. I. Packer

 **VIDEO NOTES**

In Chapter 1 we learned: What you think about God shapes your relationship with Him.
   ~ It determines how you perceive God
   ~ It determines how you think God perceives you
   ~ It determines how you relate with God

In Chapter 2 we learned: "We tend by a secret law of the soul to move toward our mental image of God."
   ~ We tend to assume God is just like us
   ~ We tend to reduce Him to manageable terms
   ~ We tend to overlook the obvious and significant
     ways He has revealed Himself to us

In Chapter 3 we raised the question: How do I know if I am seeing God as He really is?
   ~ Take the vision test on page 242 of the book and rate yourself in the following areas:
       ~ Those who know God have great energy for God
       ~ Those who know God have great thoughts of God
       ~ Those who know God show great boldness for God
       ~ Those who know God have great contentment in God

"*What comes to into our minds when we think about God is the most important thing about us. For this reason the gravest question before the Church is always God himself, and the most portentous fact about any man is not what he at a given time may say or do, but what he in his deep heart conceives God to be like.*"

— A. W. Tozer

Small Group Questions

1. If you haven't done so, take the vision test on p. 242 of the book.

2. Who do you know that has great *energy, thoughts, boldness,* and/or *contentment* for God?

3. Share specific ways you are personally getting to know God. Is it through His word? His nature?

FACILITATOR T!PS

You don't have to share the vision test scores unless you feel like your group is already transparent enough to do so. It would make a great discussion starter.

 From Head to Heart

Who did you put down as someone who has great energy, thoughts, boldness, and/or contentment for God? Set up a lunch or write them a letter and ask this question, "What are your best practices and spiritual disciplines for getting to know God?"

NOTES

God: As He Longs for You to See Him

2

WEEK TWO

The Goodness of God

There's an old story about a Chinese gentleman who lived on the border of China and Mongolia. In those days, there was constant conflict along the perimeter. The Chinese man had a beautiful horse, a mare, who one day leaped over the fence, raced down the road, crossed the border, and was captured by the Mongolians. His friends came to comfort him.

"That's bad news," they said sadly.

"What makes you think it's bad news?" asked the Chinaman. "Maybe it's good news."

A few days later the mare came bolting into his corral, bringing with it a massive, snow white stallion. His friends crowded around. "That's good news!" they cried.

"What makes you think it's good news?" he asked. "Maybe it is bad news."

Later that week, his son was riding the stallion, trying to break it. He was thrown off and he broke his leg. The friends came. "That's bad news," they cried.

"What makes you think it is bad news?" asked the Chinaman. "Maybe it's good news." The next week, war broke out with Mongolia, and a Chinese general came through town drafting all the young men. He took them all and they were all later killed, except for the young man who couldn't go because his leg was broken.

The Chinaman said to his friends, "You see, the things you thought were bad turned out good; and the things you thought were good turned out bad."

If we base our perception of God's goodness on our *circumstances* rather than His *character*, our view will always be shortsighted. This week, let's discover what it means to trust the Lord to work all things together for our benefit.

Day I ~

Read chapter 4 in *God: As He Longs for You to See Him.* How did this chapter clear up your view of God's goodness?

_____

_____

_____

_____

_____

_____

_____

_____

_____

_____

_____

_____

_____

_____

_____

_____

_____

_____

_____

_____

_____

_____

_____

_____

_____

_____

Prayer for the Week:

O Lord God, full of goodness and mercy, as I look into the face of Jesus and ponder the goodness of the cross, grant that I might

Repent of my unbelief and ingratitude, Rest in Your goodness even in the midst of trial, and Risk trusting You in every area of my life like never before.

I praise You that I live under a friendly sky, that You are for me,

And that I need never be afraid of the future because You are good!

In Jesus' name,

Amen.

Day 2 ~

Do you ever struggle with believing God is out to get you? Do you ever feel guilty for having "too much" fun or feeling "too blessed" as if God may suddenly yank it all away? How does this conflict with the goodness of God?

Every good thing given and every perfect gift is from above, coming down from the Father of lights, with whom there is no variation or shifting shadow. In the exercise of His will He brought us forth by the word of truth, so that we would be a kind of first fruits among His creatures.

— James 1:17-18

Day 3 ~

RENEW YOUR MIND

Our vision of who God is can be improved by a clear picture from His Word. Take a moment today to memorize and meditate on this verse:

For the Lord God is a sun and shield; the Lord gives grace and glory; no good thing does He withhold from those who walk uprightly.

— Psalm 84:11

"With the goodness of God to desire our highest welfare, the wisdom of God to plan it, and the power of God to achieve it, what do we lack?"

— A. W. Tozer

Day 4 ~

On pages 68-69 of the book, under the section "How Are We to Respond to God's Goodness?" Chip mentioned that we must repent of our unbelief and in gratitude. Which one do you need to deal with today?

If you have never started a relationship with Christ, make today the day you make a "U-turn" and repent from going the way of your independence and start going the way of dependence upon Christ. Romans 10:9-10 states:

...that if you confess with your mouth Jesus as Lord, and believe in your heart that God raised Him from the dead, you will be saved; for with the heart a person believes, resulting in righteousness, and with the mouth he confesses, resulting in salvation.

Chances are, if you have been a believer for a while, you've started feeling entitled to God's blessing rather than showing gratitude to God for His goodness. This week prior to your prayer times before the Lord, thank Him for five ways He has shown His goodness to You.

"The proper study of a Christian is the Godhead. The highest science, the loftiest speculation, the mightiest philosophy, which can ever engage the attention of a child of God, is the name, the nature, the person, the work, the doings, and the existence of the great God whom he calls his Father."

— Charles Haddon Spurgeon

Day 5 ~

We must believe that God has holy pleasure in the happiness of His people. Are you resting in the goodness of God, or is your mind replaying all the worries of life? Meditate on Psalm 31:19-20. It's hard to believe that everything He has allowed to come into our lives has come through hands that are kind, cordial, and benevolent. Commit to start habitually thanking Him for your circumstances and gifts.

Read chapter 16
in A. W. Tozer's *Knowledge of the Holy.*

Read chapter 16
in J. I. Packer's *Knowing God.*

The Goodness of God

For the Lord God is a sun and shield; the Lord gives grace and glory; no good thing does He withhold from those who walk uprightly.

— Psalm 84:11

"How great is your goodness, which you have stored up for those who fear you, which you bestow in the sight of men on those who take refuge in you."

— Psalm 31:19

"Within the cluster of God's moral perfections there is one in particular to which the term *goodness* points – the quality which God especially singled out from the whole when, proclaiming 'all His goodness' to Moses, He spoke of Himself as 'abundant in *goodness* and truth.' … This is the quality of *generosity.*"

— J. I. Packer

How has God revealed His goodness?

_____

_____

_____

How do we respond to God's goodness?

_____

_____

_____

Definition of God's Goodness:

The goodness of God is that which disposes Him to be kind, cordial, benevolent, and full of good will toward men. He is tenderhearted and of quick sympathy, and His unfailing attitude toward all moral beings is open, frank, and friendly. By His nature He is inclined to bestow blessedness and He takes total pleasure in the happiness of His people.

Small Group Questions

1. How has this week's study on God's goodness influenced your view of God?

2. Go around the room and give thanks in one sentence for how God has shown His goodness to you.

3. What risk or step of obedience has God prompted you to take that you have not surrendered? Your future? Relationships? Money?

 From Head to Heart

~ Truth or Lie Card ~

*Look at the appendix and you will discover your perforated "Truth or Lie" cards. There is one for each of the following weeks. On the front you will write down a lie that you have believed contrary to God's **goodness.** On the back you will find a definition of God's goodness along with the memory verse for this past week. Review it every morning and night. Keep it close for the rest of your life.*

FACILITATOR T!PS

As a facilitator, you will need to "lead out." Your transparency will set the tone for the group.

Remember, go "popcorn style" in sharing.

Be careful of the rabbit trails! People will be tempted to discuss the various views on God's sovereignty. Remember to major on the majors.

Close in prayer for each other

NOTES

God: As He Longs for You to See Him

3

WEEK THREE

The Sovereignty of God

"I'd like a drink of water with two parts hydrogen and two parts oxygen, please."

"Sorry, that's hydrogen peroxide—not exactly a thirst quencher."

"Okay, how about one with just two parts hydrogen."

"Well, don't sit near someone smoking."

"Why?"

"You'd be inhaling some highly flammable gas. Ever heard of the Hindenburg?"

"How about three parts hydrogen and one part nitrogen, would that sooth my parched throat?"

"No problem."

"Really?

"Yeah, if you like ammonia."

Water is defined as two parts hydrogen and one part oxygen. Regardless of personal preferences, scientific credentials, alternative constructs, distaste, or even disdain, you can't change the building blocks of water. Once altered, you have a very different substance.

In our culture's laboratory of tolerance, people want to mix and match their ideas about God and *hope* it turns out to be God. For many, the idea of a *sovereign,* or all-powerful God, cannot be fused with a God who seems to allow free reign on evil. Unfortunately, regardless of personal preferences, scientific credentials, alternative constructs, distaste, or even disdain, you can't change the building blocks of God. Once altered, He ceases to be God.

This week we will discover why tolerance is incompatible with the God portrayed in Scripture. Then we will tackle the apparent contradiction of a God who is both in control and yet permits terror, disaster, and extreme hardship. By the end, we will see why the defining parts of God are both unalterable and trustworthy.

Day 1 ~

Read chapter 5 in *God: As He Longs for You to See Him*. How did this chapter clear up your view of God's sovereignty?

_____

_____

_____

_____

_____

_____

_____

_____

_____

_____

_____

_____

_____

_____

_____

_____

_____

_____

_____

_____

_____

_____

_____

_____

_____

_____

_____

Prayer for the Week:

O sovereign Lord, King of all creation, Lord of all that is visible and invisible for all time and eternity, grant that I might this day

Allow You to hold the same place in my heart that You hold in all the universe. Teach me to submit to Your wise counsel and command even as the angels of heaven do so with joy and delight.

So fully believe that You are both good and sovereign that I would absolutely refuse to worry, knowing that You are working all things for my good today even those things I don't understand and that seem so unfair.

O Sovereign Lord, thank You for Jesus, who by His willful death and supernatural resurrection has defeated death, sin, and Satan, both now and forever. I confess You, Lord Jesus, as my King, my God, and my faithful Friend and Savior!

Amen.

Day 2 ~

Write down a few images that lodge in your mind detailing the grandeur of God.

_____

_____

_____

_____

_____

_____

_____

_____

Thus says the Lord, the King of Israel and his Redeemer, the Lord of hosts:

"I am the first and I am the last, and there is no God besides Me.

"Who is like Me? Let him proclaim and declare it; yes, let him recount it to Me in order, from the time that I established the ancient nation. And let them declare to them the things that are coming and the events that are going to take place. Do not tremble and do not be afraid; Have I not long since announced it to you and declared it? And you are My witnesses is there any God besides Me, or is there any other Rock? I know of none."

— Isaiah 44:6-8

It's easy to remember those images when life feels grand. But God's *grandness* tends to shrink when life's fault lines shake our world. List the top two struggles/fears in your life and consider what your response should be to these if God is both *good* and *sovereign*.

_____

_____

_____

_____

_____

_____

_____

_____

Day 3 ~

RENEW YOUR MIND

Our vision of who God is can be improved by a clear picture from His Word. Take a moment today to memorize and meditate on these verses:

> *And we know that God causes all things to work together for good to those who love God, to those who are called according to His purpose.*
>
> — Romans 8:28

> *"As for you, you meant evil against me, but God meant it for good in order to bring about this present result, to preserve many people alive."*
>
> — Genesis 50:20

Are you reviewing your Truth or Lie Card? Remember Romans 12:2:

And do not be conformed to this world, but be transformed by the renewing of your mind, so that you may prove what the will of God is, that which is good and acceptable and perfect.

Day 4 ~

On pages 83-90 of the book, Chip discussed five ways God has revealed His sovereignty to us. How have any of those means been apparent in your life?

"No doubt all history in the last resort must be held by Christians to be a story with a divine plot."

— C. S. Lewis

Day 5 ~

Let's get real for a moment. What are you going through that seems hard, unfair, depressing, or impossible? What would it look like to stop fighting, stop resisting, stop complaining, and start trusting your sovereign Father?

_____

_____

_____

_____

_____

_____

_____

_____

_____

_____

DIGGING DEEPER

Read chapter 22
in A. W. Tozer's *Knowledge of the Holy.*

Read chapter 4
in J. I. Packer's *Knowing God.*

Tools for
Life Change:

*Why do you believe in
the God of the Bible?
If someone asked you that
question would you be
able to give a well
thought out, logical
answer? Could you give
an answer without using
the Bible as a reference?
You may want to listen to
the Walk Thru the Bible
series,* **Why I Believe***,
taught by author Chip
Ingram which gives
genuine answers to
questions at the core of
human existence.*

*An additional resource
for future reading is*
The Problem of Pain *by
C. S. Lewis.*

The Sovereignty of God

And we know that God causes all things to work together for good to those who love God, to those who are called according to His purpose.

— Romans 8:28

"God's sovereignty is the attribute by which He rules His entire creation, and *to be sovereign, God must be all-knowing, all-powerful, and absolutely free.*

"Furthermore, His sovereignty requires that He be absolutely free, which means simply that He must be free to do whatever He wills to do anywhere at any time to carry out His eternal purpose in every single detail without interference. Were He less than free, He must be less than sovereign."

— A. W. Tozer

 VIDEO NOTES

How has God revealed His sovereignty?

_____

_____

_____

How do we respond to a sovereign God?

_____

_____

_____

Definition of God's Sovereignty:

The sovereignty of God is that which separates the God of the Bible from all other religions, truth claims, or philosophies.

When we say God is sovereign, we declare that by virtue of His creatorship over all life and reality, His all-knowing, all powerful, and benevolent rule, that He is in fact the Lord of lords, King of kings, and in absolute control of time and eternity. Nothing will come into my life today that He did not either allow or decree for my ultimate good.

Small Group Questions

1. Share a time around the group when you or someone you know experienced a "raw deal" that seemed terrible but ended up as something wonderful.

2. Share one new truth about the sovereignty of God that you've learned through this study.

3. Share one area in your life that you know God wants you to totally surrender. What next steps do you need to take for Him to be the CEO of your life?

FACILITATOR T!PS

Facilitator — be willing to lead out on authenticity.

Be careful of the rabbit trails! People will be tempted to discuss the various views on God's sovereignty. Remember to major on the majors.

Pray for God's grace for each person after everyone shares their areas of surrender.

From Head to Heart

~ Truth or Lie Card ~

*Look at the appendix and you will discover your perforated "Truth or Lie" cards. There is one for each week. On the front you will write down a lie that you have believed contrary to God's sovereignty. On the back you will find a definition of God's **sovereignty** along with the memory verse for this past week. Review it every morning and night. Keep it close for the rest of your life.*

God: As He Longs for You to See Him

4

WEEK FOUR

The Holiness of God

One wrong turn can make all the difference.

Have you ever been given a list of directions only to discover at one crossroad you forgot to write down an "R" or an "L"? You have a choice. You can either make a phone call to discover the right way to go. Or, as most of us do, you can make a guess based upon your gut feeling. Unfortunately, if we make the wrong turn, just to get back on the right road, we end up taking time, energy, not to mention hearing a slew of "Brilliant! Now you've gone and gotten us lost!"

When we approach the word *holy*, we have a choice to make. We can pick up the Bible and discover what the word means. Or, as most of us do, we can make a guess based upon our gut feeling of what the word means and how it is applied to God. Unfortunately, if we take the wrong turn, we are absolutely clueless as to what Peter could mean by the phrase, "You shall be holy, for I am holy." Does that mean we need to be *perfect? Innocent? Pure?* Man, who can travel down that road?

When we say God is holy, or when we say He wants us to be holy, what do we mean? This week we will learn how we have mislabeled "holiness" as it concerns God. Words like *perfect, pure,* and *innocent* are good guesses, but in reality they take us down a wrong road in our understanding of God. In our assumptions, we've stripped God of the essence of His holiness. God longs for you to see Him as He is, not as we would want Him to be. This week, let's discover the right turn.

WALK
THRU ᴛʜᴇ
BIBLE

Day 1 ~

Read chapter 6 in *God: As He Longs for You to See Him*. How did this chapter clear up your view of God's holiness?

_____

_____

_____

_____

_____

_____

_____

_____

_____

_____

_____

_____

_____

_____

_____

_____

_____

_____

_____

_____

_____

_____

_____

_____

_____

_____

Prayer for the Week:

O Lord God, holy and pure, awesome in majesty, as I consider Your perfection, grant that I might

Commit to holy ways, Think holy thoughts, Live in holy obedience, and Reject evil with a holy attitude.

Let me hear the tender conviction of Your Spirit and help me remember that You are jealous for Your holiness. Because of Your love, You see the pain our sin will bring us, and You long to rescue us. So that Your name may never be profaned in my life, You have my permission to do whatever You need to do to make be holy.

In Jesus' name,

Amen.

Day 2 ~

How does seeing God as "totally other" help us view ourselves in more realistic light?

And one called out to another and said,

"Holy, Holy, Holy, is the Lord of hosts, the whole earth is full of His glory."

— Isaiah 6:3

Pursue peace with all men, and the sanctification without which no one will see the Lord.

— Hebrews 12:14

Read 1 Corinthians 3:17. Explain why living a holy life is so important to God. How do His commands reveal His love for us and His desire for our wholeness and health?

Day 3 ~

RENEW YOUR MIND

Our vision of who God is can be improved by a clear picture from His Word. Take a moment today to memorize and meditate on these verses:

As obedient children, do not be conformed to the former lusts which were yours in your ignorance, but like the Holy One who called you, be holy yourselves also in all your behavior; because it is written, "You shall be holy, for I am holy."

— I Peter 1:14-16

Are you reviewing your Truth or Lie Card?

Day 4 ~

Look up Ephesians 4:17-24. In that passage Paul contrasts our life before Christ and our life after Christ. Unfortunately, many Christians think they can follow Christ without looking any different.

Meditate on those verses and then take some time with the chart below. First write out the three commands from Paul found in Ephesians 4:22-24. Then, commit to one application in each area.

"Holy is the way God is. To be holy He does not conform to a standard. He is that standard."

— A. W. Tozer

Imperatives	Applied to My Life

Day 5 ~

Look back over pages 118-123 in the book.
Chip talked about four key ways that we
grow in holiness: *a commitment, the way we think,
a command, or an attitude.* Which of the four do
you need to work on most and why? Pray for
the wisdom and power of God's Spirit for
life change.

_____

_____

_____

_____

_____

_____

_____

_____

_____

_____

_____

Tools for
Life Change:

The following
resources may be
helpful during your
study from author
Chip Ingram. These
materials can be
purchased at
www.walkthru.org.

*Holy Transformation:
What It Takes for
God to Make a
Difference in You*

*The Miracle of
Life Change*

Read chapter 21
in A. W. Tozer's *Knowledge of the Holy.*

The Holiness of God

As obedient children, do not be conformed to the former lusts which were yours in your ignorance, but like the Holy One who called you, be holy yourselves also in all your behavior; because it is written, "You shall be holy, for I am holy."

— I Peter 1:14-16

"Holiness is the everyday business of every Christian. It evidences itself in the decisions we make and things we do, hour by hour, day by day."

— Chuck Colson

VIDEO NOTES

How has God revealed His holiness?

_____

_____

_____

How do we respond to God's holiness?

_____

_____

_____

_____

Definition of God's Holiness:

"We know nothing like the divine holiness. It stands apart, unique, unapproachable, incomprehensible and unattainable. The natural man is blind to it. He may fear God's power and admire His wisdom, but His holiness he cannot even imagine. Only the Spirit of the Holy One can impart to the human spirit the knowledge of the holy."

— A. W. Tozer

Small Group Questions

1. In the book we talked about the two areas we struggle with the most: sex and money. Where do you believe you are at right now? What step does God want you to take in each area?

2. What is the biggest barrier to taking that step of obedience today?

3. Who could help you and hold you accountable to take those steps towards holiness?

_____

_____

_____

_____

_____

_____

_____

 From Head to Heart

> ## ~ Truth or Lie Card ~
>
> *Look at the appendix and you will discover your perforated "Truth or Lie" cards. There is one for each week. On the front you will write down a lie that you have believed contrary to God's **holiness.** On the back you will find a definition of God's holiness along with the memory verse for this past week. Review it every morning and night. Keep it close for the rest of your life.*

FACILITATOR T!PS

If the group is mixed, please separate genders before you get started on the questions.

Look for opportunities to follow up with people in the group this week in light of the struggles they have shared.

Spend some extra time in prayer for each person.

NOTES

God: As He Longs for You to See Him

5
WEEK FIVE

The Wisdom of God

Nothing intrigues us like mystery.

Except when it *really* happens.

Our eyes leap over pages of a "whodunit." We flock to the big screen when we hear, "You won't believe the ending!" Why? Because we love when a mystery is unveiled and then resolved. Think about the flip side. We let out a moan when the words flash across our favorite TV show, "To be continued." Who likes to leave a stadium in a tie? And that doesn't come close to the feelings that pound us in real-life thrillers:

- As we wait to find out if the chemo treatments will halt the cancer
- As we wonder why the pink slip hit our desk
- As we watch the hurricane move closer to shore

Mystery unveiled: *tantalizing.*

Mystery unresolved: *frustrating.*

When theologians describe the simplicity of God, they mean that all of His perfect attributes work perfectly together, in simple harmony. We describe with great clarity His perfect love married with His perfect justice and His perfect holiness. But we trip over our minds when we try to figure out how He is also perfect in His mystery. The preacher of Ecclesiastes asks rhetorically, "Consider the work of God, for who is able to straighten what He has bent?" (Ecclesiastes 7:13). The picture is one of bare hands trying to straighten curved steel.

What sweat and tears have you lost on trying to straighten out your circumstances? What temples have you rubbed raw trying to figure out how God is going to use this dreadful experience? Surely God can't know about this situation. Doesn't He see how crooked my life is? Why doesn't He straighten it out?

This week we will learn why living in "to be continued" land is not only a necessity, but actually the best thing for us. We will be introduced to another of God's attributes: His wisdom. And that's not about God's IQ. When stuck in your next unresolved mystery, remember these principles on how we can learn to *rest* and *trust* in the wisdom of God.

Day 1 ∼

Read chapter 7 in *God: As He Longs for You to See Him.* How did this chapter clear up your view of God's wisdom?

_____

_____

_____

_____

_____

_____

_____

_____

_____

_____

_____

_____

_____

_____

_____

_____

_____

_____

_____

_____

_____

_____

_____

_____

_____

_____

Prayer for the Week:

O Lord God, infinite in wisdom and knowledge, as I consider Your purposes and Your plans, grant that I might

Live in total awe and reverence for You, Feast daily upon Your Word, Ask for Your wisdom in every situation, and Trust You completely when life doesn't make sense.

Let me know Your will and help me to follow it wholeheartedly, remembering that You already know every ripple of every action throughout history, now and forever. Because of Your wisdom, You freely offer Your best in every situation, and You provide it to all who ask. So today, I ask.

In Jesus' name,

Amen.

Day 2 ~

Look at the verse on this page. In light of what you have read this week about how God has revealed his wisdom, how does Scripture prove that point?

_____

_____

_____

_____

_____

_____

_____

_____

_____

_____

_____

_____

_____

_____

_____

_____

_____

_____

_____

_____

_____

"For My thoughts are not your thoughts, Nor are your ways My ways," declares the Lord. "For as the heavens are higher than the earth, so are My ways higher than your ways and My thoughts than your thoughts."

— Isaiah 55:8-9

Day 3 ~
RENEW YOUR MIND

Our vision of who God is can be improved by a clear picture from His Word. Take a moment today to memorize and meditate on these verses:

> *Oh, the depth of the riches both of the wisdom and knowledge of God! How unsearchable are His judgments and unfathomable His ways! For who has known the mind of the Lord, or who became His counselor? Or who has first given to Him that it might be paid back to Him again? For from Him and through Him and to Him are all things to Him be the glory forever. Amen.*
>
> — Romans 11:33-36

Are you reviewing your Truth or Lie Card?

Day 4 ～

Imagine a time in your life when you were in the midst of a great struggle. Maybe you are presently in one of those whirlpools. Now that you have a greater grasp on the wisdom of God, ponder how you may view that struggle through the lens of God's wisdom. How can you learn to rest and trust in His wisdom?

"The real basis of wisdom is a frank acknowledgment that this world's course is enigmatic, that much of what happens is quite inexplicable to us, and that most occurrences "under the sun" bear no outward sign of a rational, moral God ordering them at all."

— J. I. Packer

Day 5 ~

Let's get real for a moment. What are you going through that seems hard, unfair, depressing, or impossible? What would it look like to stop fighting, stop resisting, stop complaining, and start trusting your sovereign Father?

_____

_____

_____

_____

_____

_____

_____

_____

_____

_____

_____

_____

_____

_____

_____

_____

_____

_____

_____

_____

_____

_____

_____

_____

The Wisdom of God

Oh, the depth of the riches both of the wisdom and knowledge of God! How unsearchable are His judgments and unfathomable His ways! For who has known the mind of the Lord, or who became His counselor? Or who has first given to Him that it might be paid back to Him again? For from Him and through Him and to Him are all things to Him be the glory forever. Amen.

— Romans 11:33-36

"All His acts are as pure as they are wise, and as good as they are wise and pure. Not only could His acts not be better done: a better way to do them could not be imagined."

— A. W. Tozer

 **VIDEO NOTES**

How has God revealed His wisdom?

_____

_____

_____

How do we respond to God's wisdom?

_____

_____

_____

Definition of God's Wisdom:

"The wisdom of God tells us that God will bring about the best possible results, by the best possible means, for the most possible people, for the longest possible time."

— Dr. Charles Ryrie

Small Group Questions

1. What is the toughest issue you're facing in your life right now (that you feel safe enough to share)?

2. What did you learn about God's wisdom that gave you hope or comfort?

3. What practical steps are you currently taking to gain God's wisdom? What are your best practices?

From Head to Heart

FACILITATOR TIPS

Some people may want to share their tough experiences outside of the group. As the facilitator, feel free to provide those safe environments.

> ## ~ Truth or Lie Card ~
>
> *Look at the appendix and you will discover your perforated "Truth or Lie" cards. There is one for each week. On the front you will write down a lie that you have believed contrary to God's wisdom. On the back you will find a definition of God's **wisdom** along with the memory verse for this past week. Review it every morning and night. Keep it close for the rest of your life.*

NOTES

God, As He Longs for You to See Him

WEEK SIX

The Justice of God

Have you ever seen a dog with a shock collar?

Once he strays outside predetermined boundaries, the collar shocks, the dog yelps, and the masochistic among us chuckle.

He breaks the law. He receives immediate justice. Wouldn't it be nice if that would work in our world? Let's rephrase that: Wouldn't it be nice if that would work in our world for everyone except me? Instead, it appears like so many dogs are running loose.

We wonder about God's justice when we hear of the missionary family who moves to an unreached tribe only for the mom to contract a terminal disease. And on the flip side, our fairness needle pushes to the limit when we think about the thugs of society getting off scot-free and in the process, driving a corvette. Our skeptical preacher in Ecclesiastes laments, "I have seen everything during my lifetime of futility; there is a righteous man who perishes in his righteousness and there is a wicked man who prolongs his life in his wickedness" (Ecclesiastes 7:15).

Someone has said, "God must love wicked people, because He puts up with so many of them." We all have heard that God is both just and fair, but this week we will ask why, in our world, bad things happen to good people, and what's even more frustrating, good things happen to bad people. We then learn some practical ways to relax when we wonder why God allows so many dogs to run loose.

Day 1 ~

Read chapter 8 in *God: As He Longs for You to See Him*. How did this chapter clear up your view of God's justice?

_____

_____

_____

_____

_____

_____

_____

_____

_____

_____

_____

_____

_____

_____

_____

_____

_____

_____

_____

_____

_____

_____

_____

_____

_____

_____

Prayer for the Week:

O Lord God, holy and just, as I consider Your righteous judgments, grant that I might

Learn to treasure the sacrifice and atonement of Jesus, Abandon all vengeance to You and refuse to seek it on my own terms,

Take comfort in You when life is unfair, and Remember that I will one day stand before Your judgment seat.

Help me to rest in Your righteousness and defer to Your justice. Because You are Judge of all the earth, I bow patiently before Your authority in faith and in gratitude.

In Jesus' name,

Amen.

Clouds and thick darkness surround Him; righteousness and justice are the foundation of His throne.

— Psalm 97: 2

Day 2 ~

Reread the questions on pages 151-152. Which one do you struggle with the most and why? How has this chapter helped resolve any tension or shed light on your appreciation of God's justice?

_____

_____

_____

_____

_____

_____

_____

_____

_____

_____

_____

_____

_____

_____

_____

_____

_____

_____

_____

_____

_____

_____

Day 3 ~

RENEW YOUR MIND

Our vision of who God is can be improved by a clear picture from His Word. Take a moment today to memorize and meditate on these verses:

Are you reviewing your Truth or Lie Cards?

Never pay back evil for evil to anyone respect what is right in the sight of all men. If possible, so far as it depends on you, be at peace with all men. Never take your own revenge, beloved, but leave room for the wrath of God, for it is written, "Vengeance is mine, I will repay," says the Lord. "But if your enemy is hungry, feed him, and if he is thirsty, give him a drink; for in so doing you will heap burning coals on his head." Do not be overcome by evil, but overcome evil with good.

— Romans 12: 17-21

Day 4 ~

Pilots will tell you that as little as one-eighth inch of ice covering a wing can prevent a plane from taking off. Imagine that, a massive, steel bird with big turbine engines grounded because of a thin sheet of ice.

In the same way, many of us are grounded in our life because of a thin veneer of bitterness covering our hearts. Jesus said in Matthew:

"And his lord, moved with anger, handed him over to the torturers until he should repay all that was owed him. My heavenly Father will also do the same to you, if each of you does not forgive his brother from your heart."

— Matthew 18:34-35

Take a few moments to ask yourself:

~ Is there anyone I hold stuff against, even a little bit?

~ Is there anyone I secretly talk about?

~ Is there anyone I'd love to see God judge now so I can experience their humiliation?

It's time to de-ice your heart. Let the Father take care of justice. Meditate on **Psalm 73** and seek forgiveness for the bitterness in your own heart.

"There are two kinds of people: those who say to God, "Thy will be done," and those to whom God says, "All right, then, have it your way."

— C. S. Lewis

Day 5 ∼

Read 1 Peter 3:8-17 and 4:12-19. What are some practical ways for believers to find freedom from bitterness?

_____

_____

_____

_____

_____

_____

_____

_____

_____

_____

_____

_____

_____

_____

_____

_____

_____

Read chapter 17
in A. W. Tozer's *Knowledge of the Holy*.

Read chapter 14
in J. I. Packer's *Knowing God*.

The Justice of God

"Far be it from You to do such a thing, to slay the righteous with the wicked, so that the righteous and the wicked are treated alike. Far be it from You! Shall not the Judge of all the earth deal justly?"

— Genesis 18:25

"To reward good with good, and evil with evil, is natural to God. So, when the New Testament speaks of the final judgment, it always represents it in terms of retribution. God will judge all men, it says, 'according to their works.'"

— J. I. Packer

 **VIDEO NOTES**

How has God revealed His justice?

_____

_____

_____

How do we respond to God's justice?

_____

_____

_____

Definition of God's Justice:

"Justice embodies the idea of moral equity, and iniquity is the exact opposite; it is in-equity, the absence of equality from human thoughts and acts. Judgment is the application of equity to moral situations, and may be favorable or unfavorable according to whether the one under examination has been equitable or inequitable in heart and conduct."

— A. W. Tozer

Small Group Questions

1. Share a time when you've questioned God's justice, either in your life or in the life of a person you love.

2. What did you learn about God's justice in this study to help you cope in the midst of the situation?

3. Which of the four responses to God's justice resonates most with you in your life right now? Why?

   Four responses:
   1. *Choose to embrace Jesus.*
   2. *Refuse to seek vengeance.*
   3. *Take comfort in God's justice.*
   4. *Meditate on the effects of God's final judgment.*

4. Is there a specific action step you need to take in response to God's justice? If so, write it down and then share it with the group or a close friend.

_____

_____

_____

 From Head to Heart

～ Truth or Lie Card ～

*Look at the appendix and you will discover your perforated "Truth or Lie" cards. There is one for each week. On the front you will write down a lie that you have believed contrary to God's **justice**. On the back you will find a definition of God's justice along with the memory verse for this past week. Review it every morning and night. Keep it close for the rest of your life.*

FACILITATOR T!PS

When sharing stories people can have a tendency to "elaborate." Make sure you say on the front end to keep essence of the story, but maybe not include all of the details in order to be considerate to others.

Christianity is not a solo sport. Encourage each person to have a close friend, a "Barnabas" type, who can help them walk through times of apparent injustice.

God: As He Longs for You to See Him

7

WEEK SEVEN

The Love of God

You know what happens when you leave soda out on the counter for a few hours.

Overexposure leads to flatness.

The same thing happens with the word *love*. Love. I love shopping. I love burgers. I love my team. I love that song. I love my bride. I love my kids. I love my dog. Overexposure leads to flatness.

The word *love* is like a conversation Swiss army knife—perfect for any situation. We apply it as easily to cooked cow as we do our groom of 50 years. We use it affectionately for our daughters and ardently for our favorite football team.

What does God's love look like? Feel like? Has its flavor fallen flat on you? For many of us, we react to the knowledge of God's love as we do the tax code—a cold fact of life. Especially those of us who have been in the church for any length of time, the mantra "God loves you" moved from humbling to humdrum years ago.

God wants to move us back from flat to flavorful. We will come to realize that most of the problem stems from our lack of belief in His love. We know it in our mind, but never feel it in our heart. In the process we will discover five truths of what God's love means for us that will not only change how we view God's love, but may change how we love others.

Day 1 ∼

Read chapter 9 in *God: As He Longs for You to See Him.* How did this chapter clear up your view of God's love?

_____

_____

_____

_____

_____

_____

_____

_____

_____

_____

_____

_____

_____

_____

_____

_____

_____

_____

_____

_____

_____

_____

_____

_____

_____

Prayer for the Week:

O Lord, the God who is love, as I consider the infinite nature of Your compassion, mercy, and favor, grant that I might

Grasp and accept the reality of Your love, Abandon all the things I've tried to use as substitutes, and Sacrificially demonstrate Your love to others.

Let me rely on and rest in the certainty of Your unconditional love, even when I don't feel it. Help me to see it even in difficult times, to know that it's always there regardless of my performance, and to thank You for it constantly. Let it really sink into my heart as I've never known it before.

In Jesus' name,

Amen.

Day 2 ~

On page 184, Chip asks the question, "What would my life feel like and be like if I really believed God thinks of me in this way?" He then lists five implications of God's love for us. Which of the five did you need to hear today and why?

See how great a love the Father has bestowed on us, that we would be called children of God; and such we are for this reason the world does not know us, because it did not know Him.

— I John 3:1

_____

_____

_____

_____

_____

_____

_____

_____

_____

_____

_____

_____

_____

_____

_____

_____

_____

_____

_____

Day 3 ~

RENEW YOUR MIND

Our vision of who God is can be improved by a clear picture from His Word. Take a moment today to memorize and meditate on these verses:

> *For I am convinced that neither death, nor life, nor angels, nor principalities, nor things present, nor things to come, nor powers, nor height, nor depth, nor any other created thing, will be able to separate us from the love of God, which is in Christ Jesus our Lord.*
>
> — Romans 8:38-39

Are you reviewing your Truth or Lie Cards?

Day 4 ~

Fill in the blank: I tend to believe that I earn God's love if I _____. What prevents you from knowing God's love in your mind, and gives you a tough time experiencing it in your heart?

_____

_____

_____

_____

_____

_____

_____

_____

_____

_____

_____

_____

_____

_____

"The change of which I speak is the change from living life as a painful test to prove that you deserve to be loved, to living it as an unceasing "Yes" to the truth of that Belovedness."

— Henri Nouwen

Read chapter 20
in A. W. Tozer's *Knowledge of the Holy.*

Read chapter 12
in J. I. Packer's *Knowing God.*

Day 5 ∼

How are you receiving God's love in your mind? As an afterthought or a forethought? Instead of receiving His love by faith, we tend to settle for tangible, and temporal, replacements. C. S. Lewis aptly affirmed,

> Indeed, if we consider the unblushing promises of reward and the staggering nature of the rewards promised in the Gospels, it would seem that our Lord finds our desire, not too strong, but too weak. We are half-hearted creatures, fooling about with drink and sex and ambition when infinite joy is offered us, like an ignorant child who wants to go on making mud pies in a slum because he cannot imagine what is meant by the offer of a holiday at the sea. We are far too easily pleased.

Take your journal out and ask yourself, "How am I replacing God's love with cheap substitutes?" Is it more stuff? Puffed up ego? Unhealthy relationships?

Ask for God to help you grasp His love for you. Commit to never be lured again by your own "mud pies." *Extra writing pages are provided on pages 70-71

Tools for Life Change:

Do you know that you are precious to God? You are fully forgiven, deeply loved and have great worth, regardless of your past, childhood, mistakes and choices. You have great worth because of your relationship with Christ. We all spend many hours and days trying to be someone significant, only to realize we often don't like the person we see in the mirror. Chip's wife, Theresa Ingram, has an excellent CD series, **Precious in His Sight***, which will help you to see yourself through the eyes of Jesus. This resource is available at Walk Thru the Bible or you can purchase it by logging on to www.walkthru.org.*

NOTES ~

The Love of God

But God demonstrates His own love toward us, in that while we were yet sinners, Christ died for us.

— Romans 5:8

"Self-rejection is the greatest enemy of the spiritual life because it contradicts the sacred voice that calls us the 'Beloved.' Being the Beloved constitutes the core truth of our existence."

— Henri Nouwen

 VIDEO NOTES

Five Distinct Implications of God's Love:

1. *God's thoughts, intentions, desires, and plans are always for your good and never for your harm. (Jeremiah. 29:11; James 1:17)*

2. *God is kind, open, approachable, frank, and eager to be your friend. (John 13:12-15)*

3. *God emotionally identifies with your pain, joy, hopes, and dreams and has chosen to allow your happiness to affect His own. (John 11:33-36)*

4. *He takes pleasure in you just for who you are completely apart from your performance and/or accomplishments. (Psalm 139; Zephaniah 3; Romans 5:8)*

5. *God is actively and creatively orchestrating people, circumstances, and events to express His affection and selective correction to provide for your highest good.*

How has God objectively proven His love to you?

_____

_____

How do we experience God's love?

_____

_____

Definition of God's Love:

God's love is His holy disposition toward all that He has created that compels him to express unconditional affection and selective correction to provide the highest quality of existence, both now and forever, for the object of His love.

Small Group Questions

1. Share a time when you've felt deeply loved by God. Why?

2. What is your biggest barrier in believing and receiving God's love for you?

3. What specific steps of faith/obedience are you going to take to help you experience and enjoy God's unconditional love for you?

 From Head to Heart

> [
> ~ Truth or Lie Card ~
>
> *Look at the appendix and you will discover your perforated "Truth or Lie" cards. There is one for each week. On the front you will write down a lie that you have believed contrary to God's love. On the back you will find a definition of God's **love** along with the memory verse for this past week. Review it every morning and night. Keep it close for the rest of your life.*
>]

NOTES

God: As He Longs for You to See Him

WEEK EIGHT

The Faithfulness of God

The second law of thermodynamics states:

The total entropy of any thermodynamically isolated system tends to increase over time, approaching a maximum value.

And all God's people said, "Huh??" In English: Everything in the universe is gradually deteriorating. Practically speaking, that means light bulbs burn out. Batteries run down. Cars rust out. Bodies wear out. Friends move away. Homes fall apart. And we put caskets in the ground.

It appears so much of our time is spent replacing, maintaining, preventing, and mourning. If everything is in a state of deterioration, what in this world can we count on to remain the same?

Nothing created. But it appears the second law of thermodynamics doesn't apply to the Creator. He never burns out, runs down, rusts out, wears out, moves away, falls apart, or dies. Biblically we call Him the Alpha and the Omega, the beginning and the end, the One who was, and is, and is to come. In a word, *faithful.* God's faithfulness can be defined as His constant and "loyal love" for us.

Max Lucado writes about God's faithful love to us:

> *Father, Your love never ceases. Never. Though we spurn you, ignore You, disobey You, You will not change. Our evil cannot diminish Your love. Our goodness cannot increase it. Our faith does not earn it anymore than our stupidity jeopardizes it. You don't love us less if we fail. You don't love us more if we succeed.*

This week we will discover why God is the only Person in the universe we can count on. His faithfulness has been revealed through the centuries. His faithfulness bolsters us with hope when the repair bills come in, the mirror stops flattering, and tombstones dot the landscape of our lives.

Day I ~

Read chapter 10 in *God: As He Longs for You to See Him.* How did this chapter clear up your view of God's faithfulness?

_____

_____

_____

_____

_____

_____

_____

_____

_____

_____

_____

_____

_____

_____

_____

_____

_____

_____

_____

_____

_____

_____

_____

Prayer for the Week:

O Lord, my faithful, unfailing God, as I consider Your faithfulness and remember its newness each and every morning, grant that I might

Put all my sin behind me, covered by Your faithfulness to forgive, Bring every detail of every problem to You, Abandon all false hopes and place all my hope in You, and Be zealous to tell of Your faithfulness

Let the certainty of Your faithfulness sink into my heart. Help me always to trust that You will come through 100 percent of the time in every situation, now and forever.

In Jesus' name,

Amen.

Day 2 ~

How has God proven faithful to you throughout your life?

It is a trustworthy statement: For if we died with Him, we will also live with Him; if we endure, we will also reign with Him; if we deny Him, He also will deny us; if we are faithless, He remains faithful, for He cannot deny Himself.

— 2 Timothy 2:11-13

_____

_____

_____

_____

_____

_____

_____

_____

_____

_____

_____

_____

_____

_____

_____

_____

_____

_____

_____

Day 3 ～
RENEW YOUR MIND

Our vision of who God is can be improved by a clear picture from His Word. Take a moment today to memorize and meditate on these verses:

REMINDER

> *This I recall to my mind, therefore I have hope. The Lord's lovingkindnesses indeed never cease, for His compassions never fail. They are new every morning; great is Your faithfulness. "The Lord is my portion," says my soul, "Therefore I have hope in Him."*
>
> — Lamentations 3:21-24

Are you reviewing your Truth or Lie Cards?

Day 4 ~

Open up to 2 Corinthians 12:9-10. What has been a thorn in your life? How has God shaped you through the pain?

_Great is Thy
faithfulness,
O God my Father
There is no shadow of
turning with Thee;
Thou changest not,
Thy compassions
they fail not;
As Thou hast been
Thou forever wilt be._

— _"Great is Thy
Faithfulness"_
by Thomas
Chisholm

_____

_____

_____

_____

_____

_____

_____

_____

_____

_____

_____

_____

_____

_____

_____

_____

_____

_____

_____

_____

_____

Day 5 ～

On pages 224-230, Chip listed four ways we can respond to the faithfulness of God. You probably thought of something that could fit in each category. Rather than just having good intentions, take some time to write down how you can apply in every area.

1. Is there something in my **past** I need to put behind me?

_____

_____

2. What **present** problems, pains, and failures can I bring to Jesus today?

_____

_____

3. How can I place my **hope** for the future in the One who will never let me down?

_____

_____

4. Who can I tell this **week** about how God has been faithful to me?

_____

_____

Read chapter 15
in A. W. Tozer's *Knowledge of the Holy*.

The Faithfulness of God

Yet this I call to mind and therefore I have hope: Because of the Lord's great love we are not consumed, for his compassions never fail. They are new every morning; great is your faithfulness. I say to myself, "The Lord is my portion; therefore I will wait for him."

— Lamentations 3:21-24

"God, being who He is, cannot cease to be what He is, and He is at once faithful and immutable, so all His words and acts must be and must remain faithful."

— A. W. Tozer

 VIDEO NOTES

How has God revealed His faithfulness?

_____

_____

_____

How do we respond to God's faithfulness?

_____

_____

_____

Definition of God's Faithfulness:

"Upon God's faithfulness rests our whole hope of future blessedness... Only as we have complete assurance that he is faithful, may we live in peace and look forward with assurance to the life to come."

— A. W. Tozer

Small Group Questions

1. What one thing from the past do you need to release?

2. What current pain, problem, or failure do you need to bring Him today?

3. How can you help one another make this study the beginning of a life-changing process instead of a ten-week event?

NOTE: Next week is critical to our group's success. It's the Celebration Session. We will review, look back on our progress, fellowship, give thanks, and help you develop a game plan for long-term life transformation.

_____

_____

_____

_____

_____

_____

 From Head to Heart

~ Truth or Lie Card ~

*Look at the appendix and you will discover your perforated "Truth or Lie" cards. There is one for each week. On the front you will write down a lie that you have believed contrary to God's **faithfulness**. On the back you will find a definition of God's faithfulness along with the memory verse for this past week. Review it every morning and night. Keep it close for the rest of your life.*

FACILITATOR T!PS

Someone may want to share in private and possibly with a Christian counselor and/or pastor. Allow them the freedom to approach you after the group.

Make sure you close each sensitive time with prayer.

Make sure people know they don't have to share if they don't feel comfortable.

God: As He Longs for You to See Him

9
WEEK NINE

Time to Remember

"Papa, Papa," said the boy as he yanked on his grandfather's tunic, "what are these stones for?"

"Ah," leaning down, the grandfather pulled his grandson close, "let me tell you a story."

If the children of Israel forgot about the parting of the Red Sea, they would forget about God's power. If the children of Israel forgot about manna dropping from heaven, they would forget about God's provision. If the children of Israel forgot about the fire by night and the cloud by day, they would forget about His faithful presence.

So God asked them to set up some stones:

> Now when all the nation had finished crossing the Jordan, the Lord spoke to Joshua, saying, "Take for yourselves twelve men from the people, one man from each tribe, and command them, saying, 'Take up for yourselves twelve stones from here out of the middle of the Jordan, from the place where the priests feet are standing firm, and carry them over with you and lay them down in the lodging place where you will lodge tonight.'" So Joshua called the twelve men whom he had appointed from the sons of Israel, one man from each tribe; and Joshua said to them, "Cross again to the ark of the Lord your God into the middle of the Jordan, and each of you take up a stone on his shoulder, according to the number of the tribes of the sons of Israel. Let this be a sign among you, so that when your children ask later, saying, 'What do these stones mean to you?' then you shall say to them, 'Because the waters of the Jordan were cut off before the ark of the covenant of the Lord; when it crossed the Jordan, the waters of the Jordan were cut off" so these stones shall become a memorial to the sons of Israel forever.'"
>
> — Joshua 4:1-7

Over 40 times in the Bible, God tells his people to "remember." We are a people prone to short term memory loss. If we don't establish memorial stones in the landscape of our mind, we are apt to return to lies, misperceptions, and a fuzzy view of God.

This week, it's time to set up some stones. Ask yourself, "how has my view of God changed?" More importantly, "how has it changed me?" God longs for you to see Him clearly. Let's plan on remembering the view from here on.

Day 1 ~

Read the conclusion in *God: As He Longs for You to See Him.* How has your vision of God moved from cloudy to clear?

_____

_____

_____

_____

_____

_____

_____

_____

_____

_____

_____

_____

_____

_____

_____

_____

_____

_____

_____

_____

_____

Prayer for the Week:

O Lord, our Lord, there is none like Thee in heaven above or in the earth beneath. Thine is the greatness and the dignity and the majesty. All that is in heaven and the earth is Thine; Thine is the kingdom and the power and the glory forever, O God, and Thou art exalted as Head over all.

Amen.

But the lovingkindness of the Lord is from everlasting to everlasting on those who fear Him, and His righteousness to children's children, to those who keep His covenant and remember His precepts to do them. The Lord has established His throne in the heavens, and His sovereignty rules over all.

— Psalm 103: 17-19

Day 2 ～

Take some time to remember and reflect. As you look back over those first four attributes, what images or new insights do you have about each?

Goodness:

_____

_____

_____

_____

Sovereignty:

_____

_____

_____

_____

Holiness:

_____

_____

_____

_____

Wisdom:

_____

_____

_____

Day 3 ~
RENEW YOUR MIND

Our vision of who God is can be improved by a clear picture from His Word. Take a moment today to memorize and meditate on this verse:

> *For You are the Lord Most High over all the earth; You are exalted far above all gods.*
>
> — Psalm 97: 9

Are you reviewing your Truth or Lie Cards?

_____

_____

_____

_____

_____

_____

_____

_____

_____

_____

_____

_____

_____

_____

_____

_____

Day 4 ~

Take some time to remember and reflect. As you look back over the last three attributes, what images or new insights do you have about each?

Justice:

_____

_____

_____

_____

_____

> "I think it might be demonstrated that almost every heresy that has afflicted the church through the years has arisen from believing about God things that are not true, or from overemphasizing certain true things so as to obscure other things equally true."
>
> — A. W. Tozer

Love:

_____

_____

_____

_____

_____

Faithfulness:

_____

_____

_____

_____

_____

Day 5 ~

Filled out journals will never guarantee life change. Knowledge never equals maturity; it's only gained through obedience. As we look back over these weeks, we've discovered how God longs to be seen. However, that picture will fade when the worries of this world command our attention, when the calendar fills back up, and when you come up against expected spiritual opposition in the next few weeks.

Knowing that, here is an **Emergency Game Plan** to help you take all this knowledge from your head to your heart:

1. *Find a two-hour block within the next 12-24 hours.* Maybe it's a long lunch. Maybe it's getting up extra early. Maybe it's going to a coffee shop rather than sitting in front of the television. But change rarely occurs without reflection, and reflection takes time. Once you have jotted down your thoughts, intentions, and applications, resist the temptation to formulate a bunch of new actions. Don't jump into a bunch of new activities, goals, and resolutions. You'll probably just set yourself up for failure. Remember, change requires reflection. Take 30 minutes a day for a week to pray, think, and ponder over the specific action points you feel like God is calling you to.

2. *Get the notes out of the journal.* These notes that you have taken will do little good up on your bookshelf. Whether you journal or not, it would be wise to record how God spoke to you through this study. Grab the top-level nuggets that you know you can apply to your life right now.

3. *Keep reviewing the cards.* Day by day, review the lies that you tell yourself and combat them with God's truth.

4. *Find a partner.* God never intended the Christian life to be played solo. It's a team sport. Find someone you can trust to share your game plan. Ask this person to commit to encourage, cheer, hold you accountable, and restore you as you dedicate yourself to this plan.

DIGGING
DEEPER

Read chapter 23
in A. W. Tozer's *Knowledge of the Holy.*

Time to Celebrate

God said to Moses, *"I Am who I Am;"* and He said, *"Thus you shall say to the sons of Israel, 'I Am has sent me to you.'"*

— Exodus 3:14

It is impossible to keep our moral practices sound and our inward attitudes right while our idea of God is erroneous or inadequate. If we would bring back spiritual power to our lives, we must begin to think of God more nearly as He is.

— A. W. Tozer

Thoughts and Reflection:

Small Group Time

RETAKE THE VISION TEST

1. Those who know God have great energy for God.

Low Energy/
Vague Knowledge

High Energy/
Clear Knowledge

0   10

2. Those who know God have great thoughts of God.

Low Energy/
Vague Knowledge

High Energy/
Clear Knowledge

0   10

3. Those who know God show great boldness for God.

Low Energy/
Vague Knowledge

High Energy/
Clear Knowledge

0   10

4. Those who know God have great contentment in God.

Low Energy/
Vague Knowledge

High Energy/
Clear Knowledge

0   10

Now celebrate with each other!

 From Head to Heart

What was the application that God gave to your small group? What is the passion on your heart as a group? Focus on casting a vision for what God will do next with your group. Maybe it's blessing a couple or a person to lead others through this material. Maybe it's deciding on another study. Maybe it's taking a break and helping others on a tangible level. But leave with a game plan.

FACILITATOR T!PS

You may want to ask your group before you celebrate! What was the one big lesson you received from God because of this study?

Also, find out one habit from each person that they are starting as a result of this study.

NOTES

God: As He Longs for You to See Him

APPENDIX

Goodness of God

Lies I believe about
God's goodness…

_____

_____

_____

_____

_____

_____

God's Holiness

Lies I believe about
God's holiness…

_____

_____

_____

_____

_____

_____

Sovereignty of God

Lies I believe about
God's sovereignty…

_____

_____

_____

_____

_____

God's Wisdom

Lies I believe about God's wisdom…

_____

_____

_____

_____

_____

_____

Definition of God's Holiness:

We know nothing like the divine holiness. It stands apart, unique, unapproachable, incomprehensible and unattainable. The natural man is blind to it. He may fear God's power and admire His wisdom, but His holiness he cannot even imagine. Only the Spirit of the Holy One can impart to the human spirit the knowledge of the holy.

— A. W. Tozer

As obedient children, do not be conformed to the former lusts which were yours in your ignorance, but like the Holy One who called you, be holy yourselves also in all your behavior; because it is written, "You shall be holy, for I am holy."

— I Peter 1:14-16

Definition of God's Goodness:

The goodness of God is that which disposes Him to be kind, cordial, benevolent, and full of good will toward men. He is tenderhearted and of quick sympathy, and His unfailing attitude toward all moral beings is open, frank, and friendly. By His nature He is inclined to bestow blessedness and He takes total pleasure in the happiness of His people.

"For the Lord God is a sun and shield; The Lord gives grace and glory; no good thing does He withhold from those who walk uprightly."

— Psalm 84:11

Definition of God's Wisdom:

The wisdom of God tells us that God will bring about the best possible results, by the best possible means, for the most possible people, for the longest possible time.

— Dr. Charles Ryrie

Oh, the depth of the riches both of the wisdom and knowledge of God! How unsearchable are His judgments and unfathomable His ways! For who has known the mind of the Lord, or who became His counselor? Or who has first given to Him that it might be paid back to Him again? For from Him and through Him and to Him are all things to Him be the glory forever. Amen.

— Romans 11:33-36

Definition of God's Sovereignty:

The sovereignty of God is that which separates the God of the Bible from all other religions, truth claims, or philosophies.

When we say God is sovereign, we declare that by virtue of His creatorship over all life and reality, His all-knowing, all powerful, and benevolent rule, that He is in fact the Lord of all lords, King of kings, and in absolute control of time and eternity. Nothing will come into my life today that He did not either allow or decree for my ultimate good.

And we know that God causes all things to work together for good to those who love God, to those who are called according to His purpose.

— Romans 8:28

As for you, you meant evil against me, but God meant it for good in order to bring about this present result, to preserve many people alive.

— Genesis 50:20

Love of God

Lies I believe about God's love…

_____
_____
_____
_____
_____
_____
_____
_____

GOD: AS HE LONGS FOR YOU TO SEE HIM

Faithfulness of God

Lies I believe about
God's faithfulness…

_____
_____
_____
_____
_____
_____
_____

GOD: AS HE LONGS FOR YOU TO SEE HIM

Justice of God

Lies I believe about
God's justice…

_____
_____
_____
_____
_____
_____
_____

GOD: AS HE LONGS FOR YOU TO SEE HIM

WALK
THRU THE
BIBLE

Definition of God's Faithfulness:

Upon God's faithfulness rests our whole hope of future blessedness... Only as we have complete assurance that He is faithful, may we live in peace and look forward with assurance to the life to come.

— A. W. Tozer

As so today, I choose to place my hope in you, Lord Jesus; because you have promised to "come through for me" 100 percent of the time in any and every situation forever.

This I recall to my mind, therefore I have hope. The Lord's lovingkindnesses indeed never cease, for His compassions never fail. They are new every morning; great is Your faithfulness. "The Lord is my portion," says my soul, "Therefore I have hope in Him."

— Lamentations 3:21-24

Definition of God's Love:

God's love is His holy disposition toward all that He has created that compels Him to express unconditional affection and selective correction to provide the highest quality of existence, both now and forever, for the object of his love.

For I am convinced that neither death, nor life, nor angels, nor principalities, nor things present, nor things to come, nor powers, nor height, nor depth, nor any other created thing, will be able to separate us from the love of God, which is in Christ Jesus our Lord.

— Romans 8:38-39

WALK THRU THE BIBLE®

Definition of God's Justice:

God is just. That means all He is and all He does is accomplished with perfect integrity, fairness, righteousness, and impartiality. Justice is not a standard God follows; He is the standard. Though full of goodness, infinite in love, and merciful to the repentant, God's justice demands moral equity and eternal retribution for deeds done in the body. God's justice means no one will receive a "raw deal" in the final analysis. I can trust that He will one day balance the scales.

Never pay back evil for evil to anyone respect what is right in the sight of all men. If possible, so far as it depends on you, be at peace with all men. Never take your own revenge, beloved, but leave room for the wrath of God, for it is written, "Vengeance is mine, I will repay," says the Lord. "But if your enemy is hungry, feed him, and if he is thirsty, give him a drink; for in so doing you will heap burning coals on his head." Do not be overcome by evil, but overcome evil with good.

— Romans 12:17-21